My Best Day So Far

My Best Day So Far

George D. Durrant

Bookcraft
Salt Lake City, Utah

Copyright © 1990 by Bookcraft, Inc.

All rights reserved. No part of this bcok may be reproduced in any form or by any means without permission in writing from the publisher, Bookcraft, Inc., 1848 West 2300 South, Salt Lake City, Utah 84119.

Bookcraft is a registered trademark of Bookcraft, Inc.

Library of Congress Catalog Card Number: 89-82694

ISBN 0-88494-731-9

3rd Printing, 1990

Printed in the United States of America

To Skoshie, my little dog,
who died a week after the walk along the river.

Contents

	Preface	ix
1	Responding Perfectly: My Best Day So Far	1
2	Singing in the Morning: My Best Day So Far	5
3	Climbing to the Top of a Mountain: My Best Day So Far	11
4	Working Day by Day in a Valley: My Best Day So Far	19
5	Doing Good Stuff: My Best Day So Far	23
6	Enjoying Simple Things: My Best Day So Far	29
7	Laughing a Little and Crying Some: My Best Day So Far	37
8	Being Nice: My Best Day So Far	43
9	Having Hope: My Best Day So Far	49
10	Having Self-Respect: My Best Day So Far	53
11	Doing Justly: My Best Day So Far	57
12	Loving Mercy: My Best Day So Far	63
13	Walking Humbly with My God: My Best Day So Far	69
14	These Things Plus Today: My Best Day So Far	75

Preface

I believe that happiness is not a condition to be described in the past tense—the way you felt as a child, or how things were last summer or last week or even yesterday. Nor can happiness truly be spoken of in the future tense—the way you'll feel when spring comes, or when you're finally on vacation, or when your status changes for the better. Happiness is a present tense condition and can only fully exist if today is *your best day so far*. Just as surely as it is possible for you to be happy, so it is possible for each and every day to be *your best day so far*.

Most of the insights which I have drawn upon to support this bold assertion come from experiences I had in my late youth. As a child I had experienced many happy days, but it wasn't until I walked toward the door of adulthood that I began to learn the elements of happiness. Only then did I begin to realize that thinking and doing certain things made me feel lighthearted, wholesome, confident, content, eager, persistent, kind, self-respecting, fair, merciful, and joyful. I learned that when I thought certain thoughts and lived in certain ways I could have the accompanying feelings of happiness.

If happiness is to be a part of each day, these delicate insights, which are the keys to the door of happiness, must be constantly nourished and even relearned over

Preface

and over again. They are so easily pushed aside by more demanding but less fulfilling thoughts and acts. But when we do remember and use these keys, we find greater degrees of happiness. And when we do our best to remember to apply each of them each day, then each day becomes *our best day so far*.

1

Responding Perfectly: My Best Day So Far

Let me share with you, dear friends, something from my journal: "Today is my best day so far."

"What day did you write that?" you ask.

I reply, "I wrote it today."

You question me further. "Well, when was that day that you called 'today'?"

I answer, "Today can only be today. Tomorrow, today will be yesterday, so the today that I wrote about is today, right now, not yesterday or tomorrow." And then I repeat, *"Today is my best day so far."* To understand why I say that, read on.

A Church leader once greeted me by asking the age-old question, "How are you?"

My Best Day So Far

Without hesitating, I replied, "Nearly perfect."

Seeming somewhat surprised, he goodnaturedly asked, "Oh, really! Just what is it, George, that is keeping you from being completely perfect?"

Laughingly, I replied, "I still lie."

He smiled, and I could tell that he believed me.

In our society, the most frequently asked question (by a margin of 607 to 1) is, "How are you?" Or more expertly and warmly asked, "How ya doin'?"

The common answer to this most thought-provoking question is the all-encompassing word, "Fine."

But to respond solely with "Fine" is the most noncreative, nondescriptive, unexciting, blah answer ever devised. Being just fine places you about six-and-a-half miles short of being happy.

Feeling as I do about the word *fine*, I have for years searched for a better answer. For a time, when asked "How ya doin'?" I experimented with the answer "Champion!" When that lost its appeal, I switched to "Superb." When that began to sound hollow, I changed to "Not half bad." (That is a British approach.) But never was my thirst for just the right answer quenched.

Then one day when I was feeling so full of joy that I could scarcely contain it, someone asked me, "How are you?" And without even thinking I blurted out, *"My best day so far!"* As I continued on my way, it suddenly occurred to me that I had just found the answer that I had been seeking for so long.

Let's try it and see what you think. You ask me, "George, how are ya doin'?" I'll reply to you, "My best day so far!" What do you think? Isn't that the most perfect answer that you've ever heard! I like it so well that I've decided to write this book about "My best day so far."

Responding Perfectly

Of course, responding by saying "My best day so far" is not the same as "Nearly perfect." "Nearly perfect" is fraught with a bit of a lie. On the other hand, when someone asks, "How ya doin'?" and you reply, "My best day so far," you can tell the absolute truth every day of your life.

This book is my attempt to make some suggestions, which when followed, could make today, tomorrow, and every day that follows *the best day so far*.

2

Singing in the Morning: My Best Day So Far

Do you want today to be your best day so far? Sure you do. Well, then, you've got to get going in that direction as soon as you wake up in the morning. Nobody ever won the hundred-meter race without coming out of the starting blocks with acceleration. I know that beds are much harder to get out of than starting blocks, but if you're going to have a good day, you've got to get up—and the earlier the better.

Sometimes the worst pain of the day comes in those first minutes of morning. I've soothed such suffering by sliding out of the covers and right onto my knees beside my bed, where I ask the Lord for his help. I outline in my prayer what I'd like to do during the day. I ask for help with special challenges, such as the temptation to crawl back into bed. I ask for the courage to face the opportunities of the day with gusto and with love. I thank him for the day, and after an "Amen" I head for the shower.

I sing in the shower. At that hour I don't feel like singing in the shower, but I do anyway.

My reason for singing so early in the day isn't because I feel like singing. Rather, I sing so that I will feel like singing. And when I feel like singing, I am well on my way to having my best day so far.

I go a step further than that. My first song of the day is titled, "My Best Day So Far." I made up the words myself, and I sing them to the melody of the song, "This is my country, land of my birth." The words that I sing go like this: "This is my day, my best day so far."

I haven't composed any more lines for the song, so I just repeat that line three times. By then, with both the mind-altering effect of singing and the message of that song, I've almost got a money-back guarantee that this will be my best day so far.

Of course, that isn't the only time during the day that singing can help me brighten up my day. If I'm driving alone in my own car, or if I'm walking by myself to a bus stop or to my workplace, I sing.

Church hymns seem to work best for me. Therefore, as often as I can during the day, I sing Church hymns. Singing inspiring songs never fails to fill my soul with good feelings, and good feelings are the main ingredient of a "best day so far." What happens outside of me doesn't affect my day nearly so much as what happens inside of me. I fight many inward battles that could make today or any day my worst day so far. So to keep good feelings, I sing.

Singing in the Morning

My favorite hymn for discouraging, or difficult, or dreary days is "I Know That My Redeemer Lives" (*Hymns*, no. 136). Among all the words of that glorious song, the ones that help me most are these:

> I know that my Redeemer lives. . . .
>
> He lives to silence all my fears.
> He lives to wipe away my tears.
> He lives to calm my troubled heart.
> He lives all blessings to impart.
>
> . . . .
>
> Oh, sweet the joy this sentence gives:
> "I know that my Redeemer lives!"
> (Verses 1, 2, 4.)

Sometimes I add words of my own to fit my concerns for the day. I sing:

> He lives to keep me from jealousy.
> He lives to give me energy.
> He lives to help me do my work.
> He lives to help me know I can.

It's amazing what singing does for my sometimes sagging soul. So I sing. I sing in the morning. I sing at midday. I sing in the afternoon. I can't lose for long if I'll sing. I can't be unpleasant or unkind if I'll sing. I can't give in to weakness if I sing.

I remember a Navajo girl I once knew at the Brigham City Indian Seminary. She was a favorite of mine. She didn't return to the school for her senior year.

In October, I received a letter from her which read:

My Best Day So Far

Dear Brother Durrant,

My name is Susie. I'm sure sorry that I didn't come back to school. I hope that you miss me.

As I read that, I said in a whisper, "Oh, yes, Susie, I miss you."
She continued:

I didn't come back because my family needed me to stay home and tend my little brothers and sisters. I miss seminary. Some days when I'm sitting in the hogan I get so discouraged that I can hardly stand it. But then I start thinking about seminary. I remember the songs we used to sing. Then I start singing those songs. Pretty soon I start to feel happy.
     Love,
     Susie

Those who know what singing can do to the soul know why Susie and other angels love to sing.

I know that my singing will never win any talent awards. The quality of my voice has nothing to do with the joy of singing. I found that out while I served in the army. My friend and I were the only two members of the Church in our part of Korea. During our services, the Protestant chaplain, sitting in his nearby office, could hear us when we sang. The other fellow who met with me couldn't sing well either. We wanted to sound like the Tabernacle Choir so that the chaplain would be impressed. To get some help, we prayed. Our prayers were miraculously answered. After that, angelic tones lifted us to new heights of happiness.

Several months later, I crossed the ocean and came home. I sat by Marilyn, my wife, in church. With my newfound confidence, I sang at the top of my voice. After one verse Marilyn whispered, "You still don't sing well."

My mind did some quick considering. I decided that when we had prayed and had asked the Lord to bless us so we'd sing better, he hadn't blessed our voices—he had blessed our ears.

So let's ask the Lord to bless our ears. Then let's sing in the morning and all day long. Let's not sing for others, let's just sing for ourselves.

Sometimes our singing—at least, yours—may bless others. But I think what is more important is not what our singing will do for others but rather what our singing will do for us. Singing blesses our hearts by filling us with joy. And with those kinds of feelings we will indeed have the makings of our best day so far.

Now, I know that you may say that singing just isn't —now, nor will it ever be—part of your day. If that is the case, could you at least whistle or hum or think of the words of a song? If you can't do any of these things, then I'm sure you have something that does for you what singing does for me.

Today is already well along on its allotted path. Perhaps up until now it has not been your best day so far. Let's zero in on tomorrow as our target for our best day so far. Let's plan now to get up early; to pray first thing for all the makings of a good day. Let's sing in the shower or whistle or think a song or do whatever you feel will help you get out of the starting blocks of morning with joyful feelings in your heart and a slight smile on your face. I've got a feeling that even though we are having a good day today, tomorrow will truly be our best day so far.

3

Climbing to the Top of a Mountain: My Best Day So Far

In the previous chapter we got up early and got going on our best day so far. Now let's do some remembering. Let's think back to some special days which we have had along life's way. Let's think of days that for one reason or another were up until that time *our best day so far.*

In the early 1980s, one of my New Year's resolutions was to climb Mt. Olympus, the nine-thousand-foot mountain that rises high above the Salt Lake Valley floor.

My eleven-year-old son Mark and I arose at five o'clock in the morning to make the climb. It was still pitch dark as we began to walk down the rough road that leads along the side of the mountain to the point where the trail begins. We had not gone more than a hundred yards when I tripped over an unseen rock. Despite my efforts to keep from falling, I twisted my ankle and fell forward to the hard earth. Mark, wondering what had happened, was greatly concerned. As I lay there on the ground, my ankle felt uncomfortably injured. I knew that I now had an excuse to give up and return home to bed, and that idea seemed to be my best chance for having my best day so far.

With some effort I was able to stand up. I decided to try to walk. As I did so, I found that the pain seemed to subside. I thought I'd try to go a little further. I didn't tell Mark that there was some doubt about whether we would continue. After walking for several more minutes, my ankle felt increasingly better even though I could tell that it was slightly swollen.

The light in the eastern sky grew as we made our way up the rocky road. Soon the hill steepened. I had somehow thought that we could get to the top of the mountain without ever going uphill. As my breathing began to be more pained, I realized that to get from where we were to where we were going was going to be a struggle. The switchback trail led us higher and higher. I began to wish my ankle would hurt more so that I could have a legitimate reason to return home.

We crossed a small stream and started up a steep hill. The surface was more like a creek bed than a trail. I thought, "I can't make it to the top, but I'm going to keep going just a little bit further." Young Mark, who seemed to have unlimited energy, was willing to rest as often as I needed to. His greatest hope seemed to be that I would not give up.

Now the trail seemed to head directly into the sky. After several steps my heart pounded within my chest,

Climbing to the Top of a Mountain

and I sat gasping for breath. Then, after a few minutes, I had the strength to go on. Mark never seemed to tire.

We climbed higher and higher. I kept thinking that we'd soon be to a place where the trail would level off, but it didn't. Upward and upward we went. My strenuous efforts were paying off, and I said to Mark, "Well, we've done pretty good even if we don't make it to the top." He quickly let me know that he thought we could go all the way.

His enthusiasm and desire caused me to forge ahead twenty yards. Then I sat down and panted. We each took a tiny drink of water from our canteen and continued on. By now, I found myself wanting more and more to make it all the way to the top. But at the same time, I thought that perhaps before we could get there, I'd collapse.

After much stopping, catching breath, and forcing myself on, we came to a grove of pine trees that were a considerable distance up the mountain. We had supposed that we would arrive at the top by noon. However, by eleven we were still far from that point. Many thoughts went through my mind. I wondered why I was doing what I was doing. My only hope came from the feeling that even though my body was about to give up, my spirit seemed to be soaring higher and higher.

The top of the mountain gradually seemed to be getting reachable. But then the slope became steeper. I felt there was no way I could keep going. I'd go again for twenty yards, sit down and gasp and wonder if the wise thing to do would be to give up, while Mark, sensing my desire to surrender, would say with conviction, "We can make it, Father." I'd believe him. I'd struggle to my feet and up we'd go.

We had one backpack, and I was carrying it. I finally told Mark, "I can't carry this." He said he would. I could scarcely contain my joy when the trail leveled off and we were in another grove of pines. The noonday sun bore down on my sweat-drenched, weary body. Off to the south I saw a lesser peak. I knew we could get there without a great deal more effort. I asked Mark, "Is that the one we want to go to?" He replied, "No, that's not the one we said we'd climb." I knew even before he had spoken that we weren't going to go in that direction. Instead, we each looked to our left where the highest peak looked down at us.

We started up the rocks. Now it was a matter of pulling ourselves up large boulders. Mark went first. I had to stay off to the side as rocks were falling down. The top was now only a short way away. I felt a surge of pure hope. But just as I thought we had it made, the way became the most difficult of all. I pulled myself up one rock after another. We wound our way through chasms between giant boulders. It took us another half an hour to go only a short way, because I had to rest so often. Mark, sensing we were nearly there, could wait for me no longer. He ran ahead and shouted back, "Father, I'm here and it's beautiful!" He hurried back and led me forward. Finally, completely out of energy, I was at the top of Mt. Olympus.

No one had to tell me then why men climb mountains. The exhilaration of looking down at the valley and knowing that I had made it gave me a sense of satisfaction that I had seldom known before. My dear son and I had made it and we were together on top of the world. It was good to be where we said we'd be.

After this joyous time of savoring both our victory and the glorious view, we started our descent. In about half an hour we had made it back down the steepest portion. My ankle didn't hurt anymore, but I could tell that it was swollen considerably.

The sun was bearing down on us with all its fervor. It had been a warmer day than had been predicted. I was using different muscles in my legs now than those I had used on the way up, and those muscles were beginning to give out. My legs were becoming rubbery.

On and on Mark walked and I staggered. About a third of the way down, I picked up some speed and my foot caught fast under a protruding root. My momentum carried me forward, and even though my foot came free from the root I started to fall. It must have taken me ten yards before I finally hit the earth. Rocks dug into the palm of my hand as I tried to break the fall. Mark, seeing me fly toward him, quickly stepped aside and watched me as I sprawled to a landing. I wasn't really sure that I could get up. But there was no choice—I had to get up, so I did.

The steeper part was yet to come. I had to hold onto limbs along the way to keep from falling. I had serious doubts now that I could make it. I could envision a helicopter coming up to get me.

Down we continued. Finally, we came to the point where we had to go slightly uphill. It felt good to go uphill. I thought, "George, uphill is hard, but it's when you're going downhill in life that the pain becomes the greatest."

The ground leveled out. Mark was several yards ahead of me, and I could tell he was becoming impatient. Finally, I told him, "You just take off now and head for home. I'll come along soon." I knew then that the hardest part was over, even though it was desperately difficult to get one foot in front of the other.

Soon I saw there was only about a mile to go—a level mile. As I walked along, I was so grateful that I was nearly back. Hope welled up again in my heart. Finally, I was home. I was so thrilled to be home.

Later that day I attended an early evening meeting at our chapel. Every muscle in my body ached. I could hardly walk. My face was sunburned. After that meeting I went out and looked up at Mt. Olympus. It looked different now that I knew I had been to the top. I was so deeply proud of what I had done. I sensed then that a man was standing at my side. He asked, "What are you looking at?"

I said, "Mt. Olympus."

Then, in an almost bragging way, I said, "I've been to the top of that today."

He said, "Oh, really! That's great." Then he added, "I've been up there eighteen times."

"Eighteen times," I said. "Boy, that's really something."

He said, "Which way did you go—the easy way up back?"

I said, "Well, we went up back."

He said, "That's the easy way." After a brief pause, he continued, "I go right up the face." I kept gazing up. Suddenly I realized that what I had done was no major accomplishment for anybody else, but it was only a major accomplishment for me.

I thoughtfully turned and limped away. I wasn't in competition with him or anyone else. I was only in competition with myself, and today I had been a winner. And that made me say to myself, *"This has been my best day so far."* In the days and weeks that followed, I would look up at the lofty peak of Mt. Olympus and think, "I've been up there. Not to that lesser peak off to the right, but to that higher one—the top one—the one we said we'd climb and we did." Even now when I see majestic Mt. Olympus, I'm filled with the reward of that climb again and I say to myself, "I'm sure glad I didn't turn back."

Even though the day that I climbed Mt. Olympus was a great day, today is far better because today there is a new mountain to climb. Each day's mountain is different, but each day has within its hours a special mountain for each of us to climb. Today's mountain may be an upward slope through forests of fear, climbing under the hot sun of tedious tasks or across sheer boulders of my own expectations. Or it may be down a painful slope strewn with the loose and slippery rocks of selfishness or the entangling roots of pride.

But though sometimes I must rest and gasp for emotional breath, I must move forward. And though the downward momentum of unfulfilled hope may slam me to the ground, I must get up and go on to my goal.

Just as my son told me, "No, Dad, that lesser cliff is not our goal," so God's Son, in my greatest need, speaks to my soul and says, "No, not the lesser goal of compromise, but the lofty goal of fulfillment." So on I go, and as I do so today truly becomes my best day so far.

4

Working Day by Day in a Valley: My Best Day So Far

Climbing actual mountains is good, but you can't do it every day or you'd wear your legs down to the point that they wouldn't reach the ground. So if each day is going to be my best day so far, I have to find a valley variety of mountaintop joy. Almost every day I face routine "down in the valley" responsibilities. I can either treat these assigned tasks as mundane and dull or I can attack them with the enthusiasm and determination of a mountain climber.

I'll always remember a day I once had down in the valley that symbolizes the thousands of other days I have spent and will spend there.

It may well have been the blackest, richest, smoothest three acres of farm land that has ever existed upon the face of this beautiful earth.

Delmar Fraughton stood at my side. We'd been friends since he'd moved to American Fork from Kamas when we were both in the tenth grade. I liked him a lot because right from the time he moved into our town he was really popular with the girls. And that sort of "mountaintop" experience was the thing that I longed to share with him.

As I stood there looking at the key to my dreams, Alton Stoors came walking over from the John Deere tractor he had just driven into the field. "How does she look, boys?" he asked with a good deal of pride radiating in the tone of his voice.

"She sure does look good," I answered before Delmar could think of something to say.

"You fellers still feel good about our deal where I furnish the ground and all the plants and the tractor and the trucks and the water and you do all the work, and at harvest time, we split the profits fifty-fifty?"

"Yeah, we sure do," Delmar replied.

That was our deal. Delmar and I had thought up the idea during the time we'd stayed in the Newhouse Hotel in Salt Lake City during the state basketball tournament in our junior year. We went to the Stoors brothers and made our proposal. They felt that it was fair and agreed to it right away. Since then, until this wonderful warm spring day, Old Fraught, as I called him, and I had been dreaming of the time when we could get started on making our fortunes.

Now the time was at hand to begin. Earlier in the afternoon, while we were up at the high school, we had reasoned that that day was the first suitable day for the Stoors brothers to do some plowing. So as quick as school was out, we ran out to Fraught's old car and sped along Center Street. We continued on a mile below town to the bottoms where the farmland lay on the north shore of Utah Lake. As we started down the dirt lane, we could see the tractor just pulling into the field.

We pulled to a stop alongside the flowing well and bounded out of the car. I'll have to admit that I was not prepared for the beauty of what I suddenly saw spread out before me. The rich soil just took my breath away. As I said, it was so smooth, so dark, so moist. Mr. Stoors spoke again, "I don't think that it will freeze anymore this spring. I'll order the first batch of celery plants this week, and you can get started putting them in the ground. Is that okay?"

With that he headed to his tractor. Fraught slowly proceeded out onto the field. As he walked away, I stood silently dreaming. To myself I said, "Look at that! That soil there is going to be the means of making all my dreams come true. Fraught and I will stick those plants in that soil. We'll water them. We'll hoe all around them. We'll spread fertilizer near their roots. Our plants will grow like no celery plants have ever grown. Then, in the fall, we'll cut the celery off just above the roots and put it in boxes and load it on trucks and take it to the celery packinghouse. Then men there will pay us for our harvest. My share of the profits will be enough money for me to purchase a brand new car. With a new car, I'll pull into the school parking lot on the first day of school, and all the girls will see me do that. I'll be the most popular guy in the school next to old Fraught himself."

Maybe it was the dream that made the plowed and harrowed ground look so beautiful to me. But I think it was more than that. The realization of a dream is some distance into the future. What I saw that day was not so much a dream as it was an opportunity. Nothing is quite so magnificent as to suddenly look out over a newly plowed field or a new day of opportunity.

It is a rare day when we can climb to the top of a lofty mountain and look down over a thousand fields. But what is even better, because it happens so often, is to be down in the valley looking at just one field, or even the corner of a field—a field that is just waiting for you to plant, cultivate, nourish, irrigate, and harvest it. The satisfaction of such experiences added together day by day, rather than the final realization of a dream, is the essence of everyday happiness.

Though celery prices the year before were high, our year there was too much celery. The price plummeted. Instead of a new car carrying me into the hearts of the local girls, I had to try to enter in by walking. Needless to say, that didn't work any better that year than it had the year before.

That dismal outcome did not then nor does it now, these many years later, lessen the way I felt that day when I looked out at my field of opportunity. I can still see the rich, black, moist, smooth soil. It was ready to be planted and I was ready to plant. That made that day and each day like it my best day so far.

5

Doing Good Stuff: My Best Day So Far

I had a friend named Bob. He told me that one day on the farm their tractor suddenly stopped running while he was working in the fields with it. He came to the house. His father, who was afflicted with arthritis, asked what was wrong. Bob replied, "The tractor stopped on me."

"Go fix it," the father said.

"I can't fix a tractor," Bob answered.

"Sure you can, son," the father said confidently. And then with a broad smile he added, "All you've got to do is have the confidence to try."

The confidence to try, more than talent, seems to be the thing that separates those who "do stuff" from those who don't "do stuff." And it is those who do stuff who are the ones who make each day their best day so far.

My Best Day So Far

In high school I'd never had the confidence to try to do things. I wanted to sing in an assembly. But then I'd say to myself, "I can't do stuff like that." I wanted to take an art class and paint a lovely picture. But I'd say to myself, "I don't do that sort of stuff." I even wanted to play football, but when I approached the coach with the idea he didn't seem too excited, so I decided not to try.

All in all I got so I didn't dare to do much of anything. Then one day, one wonderful day, things changed, and I decided that I'd declare my independence from my inferiority complex and start to do stuff.

Don's Sweet Shop was a sweet shop owned by a guy named Don. Don was a smart guy. He not only had a place where you could get delicious hamburgers and milkshakes, but more important than that, he also hired the best-looking girls in all of American Fork. Needless to say, I enjoyed frequenting Don's wonderful place.

I'd never, to that time, been so happy as I was one night when I reached out to open the door and enter Don's Sweet Shop to have my favorite flavor of milkshake. I was dressed a little fancier than usual because I'd just had an interview with my stake president. So, of course, I was wearing a suit.

He had asked me several questions about my Church attendance, my habits, and my feelings. After I'd replied, he said, "George, we'd like you to be an elder. How would you like that?"

I replied with great joy, "I'd like that a lot, President."

He said, "You'll be a good elder, George. I've watched you for several years, and you've been a good boy. Now you are ready to do a lot of good things in your life. Things like college, a mission, and marriage."

Doing Good Stuff

Then he asked, "How do you feel about all that?"

I felt real good, so I replied, "I've never done much stuff, President. But lately I've been thinking a lot. Maybe I'll do better."

After I'd said good night to him, I headed right to Don's. I was wearing my navy blue suit—blue is my color. And, of course, because of what had happened in my stake president's office, I was feeling as good inside as I was looking on the outside.

As I entered I noticed that there were three girls working behind the counter. As they saw how good I was looking, they seemed to sort of push and shove each other in a race to get to the counter where I'd just sat down. Finally, the one who had won smiled and said, "Hi, George."

I smiled and lowered my voice an octave or so, so I'd sound as spiritual as an elder ought to sound.

"Hi," I replied.

"What would you like?" she asked.

"Well, I'd like a cherry chocolate milkshake with more cherry in it than chocolate," I answered.

"I know just how you like it, George," she said as she hurried away to her task.

As I waited for my treat, I looked around to see who else was there. I nodded a greeting to each. As people went toward the door, I would catch their eye and say, "See you later." Up until then I knew that I had a few friends. But now I felt as if I had a million friends in American Fork alone.

When people entered, even though I was timid, I greeted them with a warm smile, and they would respond in just the same way. I'd never until that time thought of myself as being popular, but now it seemed to me that people liked me—and I sure did like them.

My Best Day So Far

"Here it is, George," the pretty waitress said as she set the overflowing, extra thick milkshake before me.

As I sat sipping the delicious cherry chocolate contents into my mouth, my mind went soaring. I was having a silent conversation with myself. Without speaking, I heard myself say, "I'll bet I could do stuff. I'll bet I could do college work and all that kind of stuff. I'll bet I could paint pictures and do all sorts of art stuff. And live good and pay tithing and do spiritual stuff, and love everybody and help people and do stuff like that. I'll bet I could even go on a mission. It would be hard for me because I sure feel timid about talking to people and that kind of stuff, but I'll bet I could. I'll bet I could really amount to something in life. I'll bet I could do a lot of stuff."

My thinking was suddenly interrupted by the noise milkshakes make when they are gone.

I called the girl over and gave her a dollar bill. She asked, "Was it good, George?"

"Yeah," I said. "It was real good. I enjoyed it a lot."

I paid the bill and said good-bye. I headed for home because I had some stuff to do.

It seemed to me that that night and other times when I get to thinking that I can do stuff that I look better, and feel kinder, and act friendlier, and walk better with the Lord.

Some days I feel down. On those days, something says to me, "George, you can't do stuff." I sort of lose my courage.

That's when I sing. Then I pray. Usually I hear a small voice say, "George, you can do it. All you've got to have is the courage to try. Get up and do it." And when I do that, it gives me confidence to do some other

Doing Good Stuff

stuff. Pretty soon I'm not only doing stuff that I'm expected to do for my work or my classes or my assignments, but I'm also doing more. You know what I mean? If I were a welder by trade, I would write poetry. If I were a poet, I'd build a room on the house. If I were a teacher, I'd put a new generator in my car. If I were a housewife, I'd paint an oil painting. If I were bashful, I'd call a girl and get a date. And you know, if I do a little stuff, and then some more, pretty soon I will have done a lot of stuff. Feeling I can do stuff and doing it makes what could have been a bad day into my best day so far.

6

Enjoying Simple Things: My Best Day So Far

I've learned that each of life's paths leads in at least two directions. Often one must go the direction of duty and pressure and stress. But if I'm going to have my best day so far, I will also need to take some time to go the other direction—the direction that leads to relaxation, contemplation, and deep, deep appreciation.

It was the summer between my sophomore and junior years of high school. I don't know what it is about summertime, but back in those days I always seemed to do my best thinking during those warm and carefree months. Perhaps because there wasn't much structure in the summer and my mind was left free to do some wonderful wandering.

Being away from the high school crowd for two

months had dimmed my mind somewhat as to how difficult it was for me to fit in socially with girls the way I desired. I suppose my lack of social prowess and having so much time to dream is what prompted me to wait on the front porch for Ronnie Clements to come by to deliver our *Deseret News*. After a several-minute wait, I saw him pumping his old balloon-tire bike up the Alpine Road. As he cocked his arm to heave the paper onto our porch, I shouted, "Hey, Ronnie! Hold up a minute. I need to talk to you." Being a little weary from his ride, Ronnie leaned his bike against our fence, walked up the front walk, and sat down beside me. After a little small talk I said, "Ronnie, don't you deliver papers to the houses on Center Street?"

"I sure do," he replied.

I then asked him if in his work he ever saw a certain really pretty girl who lived in a brick house on the corner. He answered, "Oh, sure. I see her almost every day. As a matter of fact, I'll be down there in about ten minutes. I'm sure I'll see her then." When he said that I got so excited that I could hardly contain myself.

"Would you mind asking her something?" He agreed and wanted to know what I wanted him to ask her.

"Ask her if she would go to the movie with me at seven o'clock this Friday night." He agreed, and after he had got a drink of cold water from our hose, my magnificent messenger was on his way.

The next day I was out on the porch at least half an hour before Ronnie's scheduled arrival. Finally he appeared. I was so fearful that the news would not be what I desired that I did not dare approach the subject. But before I could say anything, Ronnie shouted, "She said yes. She'd love to go with you."

Enjoying Simple Things

As soon as I heard those words I knew that I had made a serious error. Up until that time my summer had been stress free. But now, I suddenly had the makings of an ulcer.

Friday night came all too soon. At about six-thirty I set out on foot for her house. As I walked past the old Star Flour Mill, I seriously considered returning home. Conscience alone drove me on. I walked down the mill lane; walking there usually brought me toward a quiet peace. But this time I felt only disquieting turmoil.

Finally I was at her door. I knocked. She answered, and a few minutes later we were walking the last three blocks to the Cameo Theatre. We weren't holding hands as we walked. We weren't even talking. As we entered the theatre, I purchased a bag of fresh buttered popcorn. We went down the left aisle. I don't know why I did that, because always before I'd sat on the right side. I didn't seem to be able to think straight. The movie was entitled *Sentimental Journey*. I didn't know what it was about, because my mind longed not for a sentimental journey but just for a plain old journey home. I was so nervous that I didn't dare offer her any popcorn for fear she would say no. If she had rejected my offer, I don't know what I would have done. The safest procedure seemed to be to not risk rejection and to just eat the popcorn myself.

The movie seemed to last longer than *Gone with the Wind*. I've never seen such a welcome sight as when "The End" flashed on the screen. We walked to her house in considerable silence. I came about as close to kissing her good night as the Wright brothers came to flying to the sun. I bade her a quick good-bye and headed home. As I walked the other direction through the old mill lane, this time my journey brought me peace.

Life is by nature filled with things almost as stressful as that date at the Cameo Theatre. And unless we balance off those things with a walk back down the lane of relaxation, we are likely headed to our worst day so far.

Through the years, I've improved somewhat on how I handle social affairs. But I still find greater joy walking down quiet, peaceful, and lonely lanes than I do at social gatherings. Don't get me wrong; I like going places and doing things with people. It's hard to have a good day without some good social life. I also like doing really exciting things such as going to amusement parks and riding on the "Small, Small World" ride at Disneyland. I love taking exotic vacations. I also like to be involved in tasks which require me to work under some stress. But the thing that really makes me happy is to go down the path in the direction that is marked with signs such as Simplicity This Way, or Just Nineteen More Steps to the World's Most Quiet Place, or Please Listen to the Symphony of the Birds, or Straight Ahead is a Pure Stream of Clear Thinking.

I like to write books and articles and stuff like that. Writing is exhilarating, but for me it is also stressful. In a few minutes, when I've completed the rough draft of this chapter, I'm going to go home. Just thinking of that pushes my happiness barometer up about seven degrees. I'll get to my house about six o'clock.

Marilyn, who is the heart of each of my best days, will have prepared a simple meal. I'm so glad that we won't be going out to dinner. My son Mark will be there. He is our eighth and last child. The very thought of him brings me joy.

Enjoying Simple Things

While we eat, we will talk. Just to hear Mark say, "Hey, Mom and Dad, guess what happened to me today!" will be among the most joyful of today's sounds.

I'll say to Marilyn, "Oh, that was a delicious meal." She will reply, "Thanks." "And to show my appreciation I'm going to do the dishes." And you know what? I really won't mind. Doing dishes in a happy home, after a delicious meal, is a most satisfying experience for a husband. Not for a wife, but for a husband.

Then I'll say to Marilyn, "I'm going for a walk." I'll shout at my little dog, Skoshie, "Side!" "Side" is dog talk for "Let's go outside and go for a walk." Skoshie will bark with uncontainable joy and run quickly to the door, wagging her tail behind her.

We will drive four blocks to the Provo River, park our car under a big tree, open the door, get out, and head down the river. Skoshie will run all four directions at once. I will stride along the path that follows the riverbank. My thoughts will run back and forth through my mind in the same exciting motion that Skoshie's legs will take her small body.

I will see others running along the path. Some of them will have electronic radios or tape players that plug sound into their ears. I'm sure that they enjoy that. But for me, the only sound that I desire to hear is the sound of my own thoughts. I haven't counted, but it seems to me that I can think of at least seventeen hundred wonderful things in one walk along the river.

My thinking may be a little foggy and sometimes negative as I begin my journey, but by the time I cross the river bridge and arrive at the duck pond, things will begin to clear up. Skoshie used to bark at the ducks. But one day when she did that, I told her in a harsh voice, "Skoshie, if you ever bark at those ducks again, I'll never bring you on another walk." She understands that kind of straight talk, and that was the last time she ever barked at the ducks.

I won't bring enough bread to feed all those dear water fowl. Other people do that. I just bring enough for one special duck. He can't see. Even though he knows the bread is there, his most frantic effort seldom brings him success. I go over by him and drop some right in front of him so that he gets two or three pieces before the others get all the rest. Skoshie cocks her head and seems happy at the blind duck's success.

Then we will walk over to the grove of trees in the primitive part of the park. There is a little stream there which curls its way around the grass and bushes. Skoshie likes this part of our walk the best. She runs all about trying to frighten the gray birds from the bushes to the highest limbs of the tallest trees. I stand close to the tree that seems to be the father of that little forest. There I think and pray and ponder. Thinking seems to go a lot better for me when it is mixed with prayer. I don't kneel down, because other people wandering along the path might think such an act a bit beyond normal. I don't even speak out loud. I just think my prayers. Heavenly Father has good ears and he seems to hear my every word. I silently speak of people I love, the hopes that I have, and my motives that need some adjusting. I feel so much of both heaven and earth as I stand there with my mind wandering in and out of my dreams.

Both Skoshie and I hate to leave our humble little forest to start back to the car, but time finally insists that we move on. Sometimes as we walk along, if no one is there, I sing. The sound of the river currents provides the accompaniment, and I seem to sound real good. At least, Skoshie never complains.

Enjoying Simple Things

Finally, we are in the car. As I turn the key to start the motor, I say to my dear little friend, "Skoshie, was that fun?" She wags her tail vigorously, comes from her side of the car to mine, and licks my hand, which is her way of saying, "It was our best walk so far." As we get close to our street we see the white fence in front of our house. It is the fence that I built. I'm not a good carpenter, but I wanted a simple white fence, and so knowing that I can do stuff, I built it. It looks good in front of our white frame home. As we walk up the front walk, it will be late evening—time to take the flag down. So while Skoshie sort of stands at attention, I'll pull the cord and down it'll come. I'll gather the soft stars and stripes in my arms, and then Skoshie and I will go inside. As I enter my home, I'll know again that this is the headquarters of my happiness.

On other nights there will be more exciting and pressing things to do. Things like meetings and ball games and parties and movies and visits with friends. But tonight, doing these simple things with my family, with my dog, with myself, and with God will make this my best day so far.

And so my dear friends—my busy, highly motivated friends—I say to you, take at least a tithing's portion of time to go down life's daily path in the "other" direction, the direction that leads away from pressure and the public, the direction that leads to a quiet, relaxing, contemplative simplicity. When I walk that direction, even several steps, it gives a savor to my feelings that helps make that day my best day so far.

7

Laughing a Little and Crying Some: My Best Day So Far

It seems that balanced days are the best days. Best days are days when you work some, and dream some, and sing some, and read some, and do some different stuff. And of course, no day would be a best day unless one can laugh some and maybe even cry a little.

By the end of my junior year in high school, I was beginning to have some deep but still hidden desires to do some good stuff of the kind I'd never done before.

There were two political parties in our high school. One was called the "red" party, and the other was called the "white" party. That corresponded with our school colors, which were red and white.

As names were being submitted for primary candidates for student body president, I longed for someone to suggest that George Durrant would be an excellent candidate. But because the students in my school were sort of dumb and because they wouldn't allow my mother to place a nomination, my name was never suggested.

Finally the candidates were named and posters went up all over the school. All I could think of when I saw the posters was that I could do a better job than any of those who were running. The reason why I felt the way I did was that I knew I was funnier than any of them. And to me it seemed that the main qualification for a high school student body president was to be funny.

Finally, the pressure within me became so great that I could restrain it no longer. As I walked home on the Tuesday afternoon before the Friday election, I began to formulate in my mind what I would say in the Thursday assembly if I was one of the two candidates. As I walked up the old mill lane I thought of one funny thing after another. In my mind, I fashioned the funniest, and thus the greatest, campaign speech ever to be given at American Fork High School. Finally, at home, I retired to the parlor to write down my thoughts. In just one half-hour it was finished.

But what could I do with it? I wasn't a candidate. Would this masterpiece go ungiven? Could I somehow give it to one of the two candidates? No, that would be unfair to the other one. Besides neither of them had the right touch to say all of these funny things. Then it hit me with pure inspiration. A third party! A third party with George Durrant as the candidate. The excitement was almost more than I could bear.

The next day I sat outside the principal's office. My heart was pounding. A few minutes later, I was presenting to the principal my one-man petition for a third party. Sadly, my ability to persuade was far less than my fancied sense of humor. So in five minutes I had killed the third party idea.

I suppose my main regret about that fateless day was not that I never became student body president but rather that that magnificently funny talk was never delivered. The happy part of the story is that it led me to a series of other experiences where I found the advantages of humor.

I was not the most popular boy in my school. On the other hand, I was not the least popular. Toward the end of my senior year and during my freshman year at college, my popularity took an upward swing.

I remember sitting in Don's Sweet Shop with Billy Mower. As we were eating a small order of fries, I was sort of clowning around. Billy was really laughing. He said "George, you're not just funny looking, you're just plain funny."

As time went by I had a lot of friends who said, "I like being around you, George, because you're funny." This was a real breakthrough for me. I'd tried basketball and I wasn't good at that. I'd tried being tough and I wasn't good at that. But I hadn't really tried being funny and yet I seemed to be sort of good at that.

Through the years I have gotten much mileage out of having a keen sense of humor. However, I have learned that though a sense of humor is a virtue, it can also, unless used in wisdom, be a weakness. It is not a primary qualification for any meaningful task or responsibility. On the other hand, it should be a definite secondary resource for any task, responsibility, or relationship.

For some of us a keen sense of humor, if unrestrained, can cause others to question our sincerity. But if restrained, it can be the very oil needed to lubricate difficult relationships and put some inherently sober matters into a more realistic perspective.

The art of an appropriate sense of humor includes knowing just what sober situations can appropriately be lightened by a laugh. Some things are not to be laughed at. Rather they are to be cried over.

So as we face each day, we meet many opportunities and many problems. As we do, we need to discern, "Is this something about which I should laugh or about which I should cry? Is this a time to be sober or a time to lighten things up a bit?" Perhaps knowing when to laugh and when to cry is one of the greatest indications of maturity.

I do some speaking to groups here and there. I have found that people enjoy laughing a bit as I deliver a message to them. But my main motivation in making them laugh is so that I can say some deeply serious things to them. Yet, sometimes when the talk is over, some say, "I sure did like your talk. It was so funny." Such a comment greatly saddens me. It makes me want to never again say a funny thing. What pleases me is when someone says, "I love your sense of humor, but you sure said some powerful things—things that you could not have said if you hadn't had us in such a good mood."

The problem is that sometimes all that some hear is the humor. So I have to be careful. Some of the standards that I have set for myself are: First, I will never make light of sacred things. Never will I speak of God or prayer in any tone other than the most sacred way that I know how. Second, I will never use any humor that will in any way take away the dignity of myself or another person. If I make good-natured fun of anybody, it will always be me.

Long ago, I found that I could speak of myself as being handsome and that people, for some reason, thought that that was funny. I can't see why they think my saying that I am handsome is funny, but they do. My son, Matt, says, "Dad, your going around saying that you are handsome is an amazing thing." He added, "If someone else did that, it would seem like bragging, but when you do it, people see it as so ridiculous that they laugh and think it's great."

Of course, I don't agree with my son, because the reason I say that I am handsome is that I am. No one else ever says it, so I have to say it myself or no one would ever know the truth. I recall once when my son, whom I just mentioned, was on a mission. I told the freshmen girls in the college class that I was teaching that he didn't get any letters and that I would like them to write to him. Their ballpoint pens all clicked open. Then I added, "He looks just like me." At that announcement, I could hear all the pens click closed.

Sometimes I am tempted to give up my humorous side. "Perhaps," I say to myself, "people don't take me seriously. If I wasn't funny, maybe I'd be more successful." But then I think, "No, I must not give up my sense of humor because it really is part of me. If I gave it up, I would be dishonest with myself."

So, of course, for me on this issue and for you on other issues the answer is to use good sense—to have balance in all things. So I'll do that. And you do it too.

But today as we seek for wisdom's balance, let us be sure and have a few laughs, or the scales will tilt too much toward glumness. And let's make our heartiest laughs the ones we laugh at ourselves. That shouldn't be too difficult, because you and I really are pretty funny.

And along with the laughs, make sure you do some

My Best Day So Far

crying. Some things (and I don't need to point them out because you'll know them when they come), just by their nature, deserve some inward tears, and many are worthy of outward remorse.

Some days are heavy. On those days I cry a bit inside and, once in a while, outside. If you and I are sensitive, we'll be blessed with such feelings. But whenever we can, let's talk about the good things and do some laughing together. Amidst our laughter and our tears, we'll be able to say with deep feelings, "This is my best day so far."

8

Being Nice: My Best Day So Far

Whenever I'm making my way down the path of life and clumsiness causes me to trip over a tiny pile of self-doubt, or to slide on the slick ice of jealousy, or to stumble into a pothole of negative feelings about others —whenever I'm falling toward a dismal day—the best way to regain my balance is to be nice to someone. One act of niceness can turn a dismal day into a joyous day. One after another, after another, after another, acts of niceness can help me shoot down self-doubt, step aside from jealousy, and stamp out negative feelings. Being nice can give me the inward feelings that will make this day and any day my best one so far.

Finally I was alone in my room. Now, in the few minutes I had before hurrying off to my high school graduation, I'd be able to read and savor what she had written in my high school year book. I could scarcely contain my excitement as a quick glance revealed that her special message took up a whole page.

My eyes quickly focused on the first two words, "Dear George." I paused and wondered what hidden meaning might be behind such a warm greeting. Before reading on, I sat and recalled how those two words, and all the others that I was about to read, had been written.

Interspersed throughout my last year of high school I had had many good days. But this day—the day we all got our high school year books—had the makings of my best day so far.

The first thing I did was to turn to the portraits of the seniors. I scanned down to the *D*'s. There I was. I was more than pleased to see that my picture looked pretty good—sort of a real likeness.

I looked at a few more pictures, but looking at pictures isn't really what a year book is for. Its major purpose is to write stuff in.

Before more than five minutes had passed, I'd written in Bob Nelson's book and he had returned the favor. I must have written forty-five genuine heartfelt messages and received the same number by lunch time.

It was in the early afternoon, just before we were scheduled to rehearse how we'd march in for graduation, that I saw her standing with three of her friends under the giant weeping willow tree that shaded the lawn in front of dear old American Fork High.

She smiled, and that gave me the courage to ask her if she'd write in my book. I was astonished when she replied, "I sure would, if you'd let me take it someplace where I could be alone."

"You can do that," I said.

Being Nice

She took it and held it close to her and walked back into the school. I didn't know whether to sit down or go for a walk or shout or what.

Finally, in about half an hour, she came back and handed me the book. I thanked her and she replied, "I hope you don't mind my taking up a whole page."

"No, it's okay," I replied with syllables of pure sincerity.

As time went on that day, I had plenty of chances to read what she'd written. But each time there were people around. And I just couldn't read something that sacred without being completely alone. Besides, the longer I waited to see what it said, the longer I could dream about what it might say.

But now, as I said earlier, I was alone. Now was the time to read. Again I read, "Dear George." That was the first time she'd ever called me "Dear George." I read on. "I think that you are the nicest boy in the senior class." I'll have to admit I was a little disappointed that the first thing she'd mentioned about me was that she thought that I was nice. I had sort of hoped that other things about me stood out more than my niceness.

I had sort of hoped she would write, "Dear George, You are the most athletic boy in the senior class," or "You are the most popular boy in the senior class," or "You are the most handsome boy in the senior class." Of course, such words would have been stretching the truth a bit. But in a year book inscription, that's not the world's greatest sin.

Even calling me the nicest boy in the class didn't do justice to Clifford Laycock and Val Stoors and at least twenty others. But, of course, in her defense she didn't say I was the nicest. Instead, she had just stated that as her opinion.

I guess having her list being nice as my leading quality was only disappointing because being nice had never been even on my top ten list of qualities I wanted to be noticed for. It wasn't even as high as being studious.

If she had really picked out something about me that would have pleased me to perfection she would have written, "I think that you are the toughest boy in the senior class." That would have correlated with what I wanted to be.

All my life I'd wanted to be tough. Oh, I didn't want to be tough enough to get in fights. A guy can get hurt by being that tough. I just wanted to be tough enough that my classmates would say, "There is old George. He sure is tough."

"Of course, she doesn't know what tough is," I reasoned. She specializes more in what nice is. And if she said I was nice, then that was okay.

The message on the rest of her magnificent page went on to tell me what she thought a nice guy like me ought to do in life. She listed some things like college, a mission, and other things I'd not considered doing.

That was all right, but I was looking for a line or two of love. When I came to the last word, I was inspired but disappointed. So I read "Dear George" three more times and then closed the book on the entire matter.

Now, after high school has drifted back into the past, being called nice sounds good. Come to think of it, I believe the greatest thing she could have said to me on that long ago day in May was "Dear George, I think you are the nicest boy in the senior class."

I've lived up to all the goals she outlined for me on that page. The one that is still the most difficult for me is being nice. If I could have but three goals come true, one

Being Nice

of them would be "to always be nice." That is a bit selfish because being nice to others always helps me to be happy, and when I'm happy I seem to be nicer. Then, before I know it, I'm right in the middle of my best day so far.

A lot of being nice is what you say. Saying things to people about their clothes, or their eyes, or their hair, is nice. But a higher level of nice is to say things to people about what they are. I've found that I can get away with a lot of niceness by asking questions.

For example, I might see a person in the hall and say, "I've got a question for you."

"What is it?" they respond.

Then I ask, "Why do I like you so much?" "Why are you so easy to like?" "What makes you radiate the way you do?" "Why does seeing you always make me so happy?" "Why do you look so happy?"

Being nice is best defined as not only not hurting people but also in doing all you can to help them. Maybe the best definition of religion is just plain being nice.

Sometimes my children take my year book down and laugh at my picture. Then they say, "Oh, look at this. This girl wrote a whole page. Wow!" At that time I sprint from my chair and wrench the book from them. The only words they get to before I get to them are, "Dear George, I think you are the nicest boy in the senior class." How I hope that that is what will also be said of them! For then I will have the joy of knowing that my children will have many days that will be their best day so far.

9

Having Hope: My Best Day So Far

If you had been there as Adam and Eve left the comfort, security, and easy life of the Garden of Eden to go into the difficult and sometimes painful world, you might have heard them say, "This is our best day so far."

On that day, as they walked out among the thorns and the thistles and the sweat, they had something that might have made that day their best day so far. You see, they had hope. For reasons that you and I understand, they had never met a bishop, a social services counselor, or even a friend to tell them, "Adam and Eve, don't be discouraged. Things will be all right." Instead, as they walked toward hardship, they received their hope from God. In his way he told them that all would be well.

My Best Day So Far

God does the same for us. He lets us know that if we will keep going all will be well. There is no greater message than that recorded by Isaiah which has become the verse of a hymn: "Fear not, I am with thee; oh, be not dismayed, For I am thy God and will still give thee aid. I'll strengthen thee, help thee, and cause thee to stand." (*Hymns*, no. 85; see also Isaiah 41:10.)

Someone said to me, "George, I can see how some days, one every once in a while, can be a best day so far. But some days just don't qualify. Days of tragedy, sorrow, hurt, failure, discouragement—surely those days are not best days."

"I know what you are saying," I reply, "and I agree, but at the same time, I disagree."

You see, a best day so far sometimes wears a disguise. Sometimes it takes time for the disguise to fall away. And then as we look back, we see that that day—that day of sorrow, pain, and disappointment—was a day of great learning. It was a day that could only be endured because of hope.

But hope is so delicate. It is one of the tenderest of all feelings. What if it dies? Then what? That question isn't worth considering, because hope never dies. It is always there. God will see to that. Maybe it will be a flicker so small that it can only be seen on the darkest of nights and in the saddest of experiences. But it is still there. Its small flame needs only to be fanned. That is why having hope is only surpassed as an ingredient of happiness by the joy-filled process of giving hope to others. And any day filled with inward hope—even a tiny bit of hope—or a day when you fan the hope of others, is indeed the best day so far.

I wanted to be a star basketball player, but I ended up on the bench. Some guys can sit on the bench and laugh and enjoy watching the cheerleaders. But for me, sitting on the bench was pure failure. It was almost more than I could bear. All that saved me was a feeling that would not die, a feeling that someday things would change and I'd be a star. I lived on that little pilot light of hope.

Toward the end of a lopsided game, some of my classmates would mockingly shout, "Coach, put George in." Their words were like water that nearly doused my hope. I'd want to disappear when they'd do that. I would pray that the coach would put me in the game, but the Lord didn't seem to care if our team lost so he wouldn't inspire the coach to call out my name. So I'd sit there.

My prayers remained unanswered—at least, they weren't answered in the way I wanted. But thinking back, I know the Lord was with me: he let me know how it felt to sit on the bench, to feel like a failure, to want to disappear, and to just barely hang on to a thread of hope. In our town he placed a few people who knew how I felt. One was Mr. Boley who ran the meat market. Mr. Boley would seek me out. He'd say things that would give me hope. He'd say, "George, I don't know why the coach doesn't play you. You are by far the best player on that team." Oh, it's wonderful to hear someone say nice things when you can hardly stand up to face another day. The Lord does so much for our foundation of hope, and to add to that he sends me to you one day to give you hope and then another day he sends you to me to give me hope.

So maybe the Lord did answer my prayers. He taught me that the only thing that even comes close to the good feelings that come when someone gives your hope a boost is to give a boost to the delicate and dim hope of another.

The Lord taught me by letting me sit on the bench that the important thing in life is to find people who are sitting on life's dismal bench and then say to them, "Come on, I'll help you stand up." Perhaps they will say, "Why? What's the use?" And you can reply, "Because I love you. I need you. And so do others. And because you're great. That's why."

Maybe when someone says to you, "Have a nice day," what they are really saying is, "Have a day filled with hope and a day of giving hope to others." Go forward today by adding fuel to the flame of hope that burns too little in a friend, a family member, or even a stranger. If we have such a day of fanning hope, it will go a long way toward making that very day our best day so far.

10

Having Self-Respect: My Best Day So Far

Having my best day so far doesn't have much to do with what other people think of me, but it seems to have everything to do with what I think of myself. As for the opinion of others, that was the most powerful influence on me while I was in high school. What I thought my friends thought of me determined whether that day was my best day so far. Finally, a true friend said to me, "George, you wouldn't wonder what other people think of you if you knew how seldom they ever do."

Whether my friend was right or wrong doesn't matter much. As I said a little earlier, what someone else thinks about me is not the driving force for me that it once was. The real factor for me in having a best day is what I think of myself. You see, try as I might to not do so, I still think of myself real often. As a matter of fact, I think about myself more than I think about any other subject. I'm not admitting that I think of myself above others. I'm just saying that I constantly have in my mind an opinion of myself. If that opinion is favorable, then I feel happy. If my opinion of myself is less than favorable, I feel unhappy. I believe that were it possible for me to gain the applause of the entire world and at the same time not be able to inwardly applaud myself, I would not be happy.

There is no more beautiful spot in all the world than Saratoga Swimming Resort on an August night with a full moon. I was there one night long ago. Just a little more than two years had passed since high school graduation. A large group of my former classmates and some others were there for a swim in the naturally hot water of the two big pools. Then we all gathered for a picnic.

I moved away from the group and stood alone under the giant cottonwood trees. The moon gave a special illumination to the lush green leaves that danced in cadence due to the slight warm summer breeze.

A young lady who had gone to a car to get her sweater saw me standing alone. She came over. For a few seconds, we stood together in silence. Then she spoke, "Quite a party, isn't it?"

I replied, "Yeah, it sure is."

After another long pause, she spoke again, "You don't drink beer, do you, George?"

"No," I replied in an almost inaudible voice. Then as she looked at me in silence, I sort of felt the need to repeat a little louder, "No, I don't."

I looked away from her and gazed out across the dark calm waters of Utah Lake. On a far shore, I could see the

Having Self-Respect

reflection of the burning flame of the distant steel mill. She spoke again with a tone of deep sincerity, "George, I sure do respect you."

With that she quickly departed and I stood alone. Over and over again in my mind I heard her words, "George, I sure do respect you."

To myself, I gently whispered, "I respect me too." And as I stood there on that moonlit night, I had an inward feeling of self-applause. It was not haughty applause; it was not proud applause. It just seemed to be respectful applause—applause which only I could hear; applause which caused me to take a little inward bow; applause which satisfied my soul.

Often I have habits, thoughts, or motives that I can't inwardly applaud. If I'm satisfied with such a situation then I can rest assured that I'm headed toward one of my worst days so far. But if I'm willing to strive for a change by singing, by standing up and walking among others and helping one of them to stand up, by being nice, by giving hope to another, by feeding a blind duck, by walking along the river, or by praying and thinking in a grove, then I can always give myself at least a small round of inward applause. And that silent sound within me causes me to want to inwardly shout to myself, "This is my best day so far."

11

Doing Justly: My Best Day So Far

I guess the reason why justice is difficult to achieve is that when it is applied it makes for a little pain for both parties involved, and even seems to be a main ingredient for a worst day so far.

I'd never played for a state championship before so naturally I was pretty keyed up about it. The American Fork National Guard team had won four straight softball games and now was poised to play for "all the marbles."

The games thus far had been played in the early evening, but the finals were scheduled for Saturday afternoon. Just prior to the time when we were scheduled to take the field, one of our battalion officers advised me

My Best Day So Far

that I was assigned to pick up the food rations for Sunday. I told him that I'd attend to it right after the game. He replied, "That won't do. It will be too late."

I answered that I'd get the supply clerk to take care of it. He replied, "No, as the supply sergeant you must be there personally."

I said, "Come on, Captain. You know about the game. We've played hard to get to the finals, and I need to be at first base. The team is counting on me and I want to be there."

"I know that, Sergeant Durrant, but the men have to eat and that is a lot more important than any ball game. So you be there."

Of course, I was beside myself with disappointment. I didn't know what to do. I felt that I had to follow the order, but the game—I just couldn't miss the game. Besides, the supply clerk would be happy to get the rations. And maybe the game would be over in time so that I could get them myself. It just didn't seem necessary for me to miss the big game.

I mentioned the dilemma to some of my teammates, who said, "Hey, he knew about the game. He could have easily worked things out. Let your clerk do it. He can."

The appeal of the game was too great. I was there. I played well and we won. After the game I checked with the clerk, and to my relief I found out that he had obtained the rations. So all was well.

Monday morning I received word that the captain wanted to see me. I walked to his office with no fear because it seemed to me that the matter had concluded with no harm being done.

He greeted me in a most amiable manner and put me at ease. Then, as he looked me in the eye, he said: "Ser-

Doing Justly

geant Durrant, I was very disappointed in you Saturday. You've always come through for me and I've been one of your greatest supporters, but Saturday you disregarded my order."

"Sure," I replied, "but I worked things—"

"Don't interrupt," he said sternly. "I'm not interested in excuses. I know we got the supplies, but that was because the camp supply officer called and said the supply clerk, and not the sergeant, was there. I told him to let the clerk have the rations. He did it, but it made me look foolish."

After a long pause, he said, "What do you think we ought to do about this? We can't just let it go, you know."

I felt that he was making a big issue over a little thing, but I didn't feel that I should tell him what I thought.

As I was thinking, he said, "I've decided to give you a choice. First, you can write and submit to me an official apology, or you can be reduced in rank to private."

I couldn't believe that he would reduce my rank. There wasn't a man at summer camp who had worked harder than me. I felt irritated.

"I'm sure the written apology would be the way to go," he said softly. "Get it done tonight and submit it to me tomorrow morning. Will that be all right?"

I sat in silence. I just didn't feel that I could apologize.

"Well?" he said in a questioning tone.

"Sir," I replied, "you knew about the ball game, and you knew that with your help the clerk could get the rations. Why are you making such a big deal out of this?"

"It's always a big deal when orders are disobeyed."

"I know that, but in this case it just doesn't make sense, and I can't feel good about apologizing. I can't do it, sir. I just can't."

My Best Day So Far

He looked at me and I returned his stare.

After a few seconds, he said: "You leave me no choice. I'll start the proceedings for you to be reduced in rank." Then he smiled and added, "I was thinking of reducing you to private. But instead"—he paused and my hopes soared—"because you are a first-class fellow, I'm going to reduce you to private first class."

With that he laughed and stood up. He came around the desk and shook my hand. As he did so he said: "I like you, Durrant. I like you more than you'll ever know." I could see his eyes moisten as he looked into mine.

"I like you too, Captain."

As I departed I could not remember all that had happened. All I could remember was the look on his face—the hurt look. I sensed that the pain he felt was not because I had disobeyed the order but rather because he had had to punish me.

That night I walked out under the stars that shone down on Camp W. G. Williams. I wondered if it was too late to apologize, but then I thought, "No, I still don't feel like I should do that." Besides, maybe the captain had done the fairest thing after all. I still had a lot to sort out about that experience. Only time would help me to fully understand all that had happened. But somehow I sensed that the captain, with his kind, love-filled justice, had done the right thing.

How do you feel about this story? Whose side are you on? I know that you think I'm a good guy and you don't really even know the captain. Plus, I wrote the story, so it is likely a bit prejudiced toward my side.

But if you're on my side, I'm disappointed in you. I believe the world needs more people like the captain, more people who don't let mercy rob justice.

Doing Justly

The easy thing for him to do would have been to say: "I've thought it over, and I'm probably being a little hard on you. I know how much the game meant. I can see why you don't want to apologize. I know you won't disobey me again. So let's forget the entire matter."

If he had done that, neither he nor I would have had our best day so far.

My tendency, and I feel you are a lot like me, is to not hold fast when someone's best interest would be served better not by mercy but by justice. It's not every day that we nonjudges need to administer justice, but when such a day comes I hope I'll have the strength of the captain. I hope I'll look not at the day at hand but at the days that are to come. I hope that I will be willing to be fair but firm today so that I might help someone have a future filled with best days so far.

Mercy is the best solution usually, but some days only justice will do. Painful as it may be to both me and someone else, justice alone will be able to make that particular day the best day so far.

12

Loving Mercy:
My Best Day So Far

In this chapter, let's look together at one of the most beautiful principles of our human experience—mercy. Just saying that word causes my soul to vibrate with joy. Life would be unbearable were it not for mercy. I, like you, want to do the right thing in every circumstance, but things don't always work out and I do dumb things, not because I'm bad, but just because sometimes I don't think straight. Then when I'm feeling so bad that I can hardly stand it, someone shows me some mercy, which makes all the difference. The following story is one of many in which mercy has given me a new lease on life.

The old Chevrolet made it beyond the Point of the Mountain, but as we passed the Utah state prison it sputtered some. Nothing worked very well in the motor of the ten-year-old four-door, but at least it ran. That was more than could be said for the heater. It didn't work at all. That had been all right in the summer and fall, and even in the early winter. But the bitterly cold January temperatures made travel painful with only cold air surging up through the floorboard cracks.

We surely wouldn't have made such a journey on winter's coldest day unless we had to. How else could we join the navy than by going to the naval recruiting office at Fort Douglas?

As we rode along, I kept wondering if I was doing a wise thing. I said to myself, "The navy—four years." That thought seemed as cold to me as the toes in my leather shoes. But what was the alternative—college? I'd tried that and I seemed to be going downhill there. Besides, if I didn't join the navy, I'd be drafted into the army. It seemed to me that the navy was better because the sailors' uniforms seemed more appealing to me than those of the soldiers. That sound reasoning added to my conviction that I was indeed doing the right thing.

Dutson was driving because it was his car. He had warned us about the heater and said that if we complained we could get out and walk. Berry had wanted to be in the navy since high school. He had sort of been the recruiting officer who had put this sea-going idea in our heads. Beano was in the National Guard already, but that was at home, and he wanted to see a little more of the world than American Fork, Lehi, and Pleasant Grove. Bago was my best friend and wanted no part of the infantry. Fraught was the athlete and was ready for any new adventure.

As the cold air turned our ears a sort of blue, we all tried to say funny things to keep our minds off our suffering. I didn't say much, because this whole idea still seemed to me a bit less than magnificent. That's why I hadn't discussed it with Mom and Dad. I had just announced it to them as I went out of the door. Before they could question me, I was in Dutson's waiting car. I could tell it hurt Mom a lot.

Mom always had these ideas of what I was going to be. Never even in the corner of her visions had she seen me on a ship or in a navy suit. That bothered me, but I'd sort of gotten used to disappointing her—and also disappointing myself.

I'm sure the idea of the navy would have been all right if I'd talked it over with my parents and others and if I'd really decided that that was what I wanted. But to take such a step on a twenty-four-hour whim unsettled my soul.

But the others seemed happy about our purposeful journey, so I tried to stay in step.

At last we were in South Salt Lake and were traveling east toward Fort Douglas. It appeared that we would make it with only minor frostbite. Just seeing the military barracks and other buildings gave me an even more uneasy feeling. Could I leave Mom and her cooking and my room to live away from home for four years? I couldn't bear the thought. Yet I couldn't turn back. What would my friends say? What would I say? "I didn't follow through on this either." I'd said that enough already.

Now we were seated inside, filling out what seemed like thousands of papers. We were told to prepare for our physicals. At the first station I heard one of the medics say to another, "We've got to fail some of these guys. The higher command says we are too lenient."

An hour later as we all sat waiting for further word, a medic entered the room. "Men," he said, "I've got some bad news. Three of you didn't pass the physical.

Durrant, your leg needs attention; Bago, you don't weigh enough to match your height; and Beano, you are too heavy to meet navy standards."

Berry, Fraught, and Dutson had made it. They tried to contain their joy. The other three of us attempted to conceal our disappointment. In doing that, all succeeded quite well.

On the journey home, we three who had failed were told by the jovial three who had made it, "You guys will end up in the infantry while we are out sailing the seven seas." I'd never in my life felt like such a failure. I hadn't wanted to go into the navy, but to be rejected by them seemed like the last straw.

When the battered Chevrolet rolled to a stop out in front of our old adobe house, I slowly crawled out. I surely wasn't coming home as a war hero. I felt what I thought must have been the feelings of a coward.

Mom, having heard the car pull up, opened the front door of our home. I entered and took off my heavy coat. I wanted to stand by the coal stove and get warm, but more than that I wanted to be alone. I walked quickly across the large kitchen toward my bedroom.

"When do you leave for the navy?" Mom asked with a fearful tone.

"I don't leave to go nowhere," I said with a voice that was just one degree short of tears.

"Why?"

"'Cause. They don't want me." With that I closed the door and climbed into bed with my clothes still on.

I didn't pray in the usual manner, but my very breath seemed like a petition of desperation to both heaven and earth.

The bedroom door slowly opened and Mom entered. She sat down beside where I lay. For quite a while she

Loving Mercy

sat in silence. Finally she spoke, "George, I want you to go back to school."

"School," I replied, "I tried that. I don't know what I want to be. So what good is school? I don't know anything. What's the use anyway."

"I've got some money. I'll get some more. I'll help and so will Dad. You'll do better. You could learn to be an artist or a writer."

I didn't answer. Why didn't Mom ever give up? I'd given up. Why couldn't she? Oh, how I loved her! She was always there. But never had her presence been so vital as it was now.

Finally I spoke, "Spring quarter starts in about two months. I could earn some money by then. I could join the National Guard. That's what Beano wants me to do." With each word I spoke, and each tearful nod of Mom's approval, hope was pushing out my despair.

"Supper's ready, George. Why don't you come and eat?"

I didn't answer, but it sure did seem like a good idea. I'd need a lot of strength for the good things that lay ahead.

As I ate with Mom and Dad, I got that deep-down feeling that this was my best day so far, and I could tell Mom and Dad felt the same way.

I guess it's easy for mothers to show mercy. They get to do a lot of that when they have a child like you or me. They tell me that mother's milk is good for a baby. I can tell you firsthand that mother's mercy is essential for teenagers. The world seems to have a multitude of methods of smacking us with justice. I suppose that is why the Lord was so generous in filling mothers with mercy.

So when life gets a little tough because someone lets you down or offends you, be merciful. Once in a while when you know somebody needs it, you could sort of let them have it with justice. But usually, almost always, be merciful. And when you receive mercy—or even more so, when you extend mercy—it will be your best day so far.

13

Walking Humbly with My God: My Best Day So Far

The temptation for most of us is to develop our personality to be clever and humorous. But in those moments when I shed such traits and just relate sincerely and humbly with people, I get the quiet inward satisfaction that makes those moments the special ingredient of my best day so far.

When I was a senior at American Fork High School, I knew a girl. She was a most beautiful girl. But although she had been my classmate for twelve years, I cannot now nor could I then really describe what she looked like. What made her so beautiful was not the way she appeared, but who she was. To me, she was like a vision: whenever I saw her or even considered her in my heart, I was lifted far above my ordinary thoughts and feelings.

In those days my outward behavior was governed by the deflated role that I had cast for myself many years before. But she always caused me to see myself not as I was but, almost mysteriously, as how I knew that I could somehow be.

In my most inward, never-disclosed thoughts and feelings, I found great satisfaction in knowing that this outgoing, achieving, dynamic, respected, beautiful person was my girlfriend. Of course, she didn't know she was my girlfriend, because I never really announced it to her. And I surely didn't want to give my friends the kind of laugh they would have were I to tell them that she was mine. So it remained my most edifying secret.

But now, during the cold winter months of my senior year, my soul was being stirred by deep-down and very small ideas that I was not to remain a dud. Occasionally, my personality would be nudged to do something slightly delightful. She seemed to notice these rare manifestations of the real me. Perhaps that is what prompted her to use her position as an editor for the mimeographed, two-page school paper to send an almost secret message to me. As I recall, it said, "What girl who works on this paper would like to ride on George's sleigh at the annual senior sleigh ride?"

The school papers were passed out during Mr. Hap Holmstead's first-hour American Problems class. Three of my friends, reading this exciting edition, got to the secret passage first. Whispering back and forth, they made such a disturbance that Hap told them to keep it down. But by then, I saw what they'd seen. I was quite pleased. A minute or so later when the girl behind me told me that she knew who the secret girl was, I didn't

Walking Humbly with My God

have the courage to ask for further details. But even though I didn't ask, she couldn't withhold the information and whispered the name.

I couldn't believe it. All my dreams suddenly came true. My heart pounded and I thought it would explode. Over and over again I thought, "This is my best day so far!"

Later in the day I saw her. It took some real courage to ask her, something that in social matters I had in short supply. But encouraged by some of her friends, who assured me that my request would not be rebuffed, I ventured. "Oh, yes," she replied. "I'd love to."

"Wow!" I thought. "Wow!"

My sleek sleigh was just two years old, and it was quite long. I got it out of the shanty that was attached to our house and polished up the runners.

Finally, the night that promised to be my "night of nights" arrived. We seniors were all to meet at the high school. I'd agreed to meet her there because the school was halfway between her house and mine. I was a little late getting there because I'd had a hard time finding my mittens. As I walked up carrying the sleigh, she broke loose from a bunch of classmates and walked toward me. When she was just a yard or so away, she melted my heart by saying, "Hi, George."

Soon we were in the big truck that was to transport us up American Fork Canyon. It was crowded because we had a lot of seniors in our class. That, plus the sleighs, made for a full load, so naturally I was sitting quite close to her. I liked that but at the same time it made me nervous. I wasn't good at talking to girls, and especially not to her.

I was glad when we got up past the cave camp and were near the ranger station. As soon as the truck ground to a halt, everybody clamored to get out and start the exciting journey down the ice-covered canyon road.

I carried the sleigh and laid it gently down. I didn't exactly know how to sleigh ride with a girl on the sleigh. As I stood there thinking, she said, "Get on and I'll ride behind." So I did, and she did, and we were off. I hoped maybe the journey would take three or four weeks.

We had only gone about twenty-five yards and were just picking up a little speed when suddenly, for some unknown reason, we were sliding down the ice on our sides, then on our backs, and then head over heels. Finally we slid to a stop. "Oh," I said apologetically, "I'm sure sorry." She was gracious but did admit that she felt a bit of pain in her knee.

I helped her to her feet, and we cautiously recovered the sleigh which had crashed upside down into a snow drift at the edge of the road. I soon discovered that one of the runners had snapped—and with it, my dream was also broken.

Disappointed, we silently carried the sleigh back to the truck. The driver was in the cab. There were two senior girls in the back. They were sitting on the straw and were covered by blankets to stay warm. We joined them.

She and I sort of sat close again to stay warm. As we did so, I felt a bit less sorry that the sleigh had failed. The two girls asked me what I was going to do after high school. I replied, "I think I'll be a movie actor like Gary Cooper." They laughed and so did she. I sort of relaxed, and somehow the conversation turned more serious. I was doing most of the talking, which was highly unusual for me, and they were all listening. It seemed as if they were hanging on my every word—especially the one sitting close to me.

I'd never talked like that before. Even though I'd felt like it, I'd always kept such tender feelings inside. Now I was saying how I felt deep in my heart. I was saying things with sincerity and with no desire to be clever.

I told them about my mother and my family, about how I felt about the Church and how I felt we ought to treat other people. Sometimes, I'd amaze myself with what I was saying. If I paused at all, they'd ask me questions. I watched the way she would listen and the way she'd look at me. I could tell the other two girls were sort of wishing that they had asked to be on my sleigh.

I wish I could tell you all that I said that night, but of course I can't really recall every word. But I'll never forget how I felt. I felt refreshed, as you do when you tell someone whom you love how you feel about the things that you love.

For the first time in my grown-up years I was me—the me that she brought out in me. All too soon the driver started up the truck. A few minutes later we were grinding down the canyon in low gear to pick up the successful sleigh riders. They had had quite a thrill coming down that old canyon at breakneck speed. But I had had the greatest thrill of all. I had unlocked a door to a room in my heart that had been locked too long and that could never be fully closed again.

Through Micah, the Lord said, "Walk humbly with the Lord." On that sacred occasion I was doing that. I wasn't ahead of him trying to be clever. I wasn't lagging behind him to the point that I did not dare to speak of good things. I was right at his side, and he was right at mine. And on that cold and yet warm night I experienced feelings that caused my soul to rejoice.

As I speak of these things, I realize that there is a time to be clever, a time to be funny, and even a time to goof off a little. But there are so many times when we just need to relate to others by walking and talking and feeling with the Lord, to not remain silent when something needs to be said, to not rush to impress others with quick wit, clever observation, or fine-tuned humor.

Never do I come so close to heaven as when I walk humbly with the Lord and say those things that he puts into my heart and do the things that he prompts me to do.

I'm sure glad that my sleigh broke down on that winter's night so long ago. I'm glad that in the truck I was able to feel things in my heart. I'm glad that I could say them to people whom I loved and that they were received in the spirit of sincerity and truth.

That night when I spoke about the good things of life to people that I loved was a good day for me. As a matter of fact, whenever I've had that sort of experience it has made that day my best day so far.

14

These Things Plus Today: My Best Day So Far

Today I walked into my supervisor's office. He casually asked me, "How ya doin'?"

I replied, "It's my best day so far!"

Suddenly I had his complete attention. He seemed shocked by my reply.

"Your best day so far?" he restated in a questioning tone.

"That's right," I quickly and confidently replied.

Now he had another question. "How old are you, George?"

I told him my age. He began to write on a piece of paper on his desk, and as he did so he muttered, "That means that you have lived 365 days a year for that many years." Finally, when he had finished his calculations, he spoke again. "That means you have lived 21,170 days. And you stand there and tell me that this is your best day so far?"

"That is right," I assured him.

I sensed that he was not convinced that I was telling him the truth. I, of course, knew that it didn't matter whether he believed me. All that mattered was that I believed myself.

Some ask me, "How can you say that this is your best day so far? What about your wedding day? Wasn't that a better day than today?"

I reply, "I still and will forever have my wedding day and the joy of my dear Marilyn." And I'll have the day when my first child was born. I'll always have the day when the sleigh runner broke and I talked to those I loved about good things and found who I really was. I'll always have the day when I was drinking a milkshake in Don's Sweet Shop and realized that I could do stuff. I'll always have the day when I fed the blind duck. I'll always have the day when my son and I made it all the way to the top of Mt. Olympus and looked down on our wonderful world. I'll always have the day when I saw the newly plowed, black, damp, fertile, rich soil just waiting for Fraught and me to go to work and make our fortunes. I'll always have the day when I read in my school year book the words of the school's classiest girl that I was the nicest boy in the senior class. I'll always have the night when I learned that hope was the foundation upon which I could build a dream. I'll always have the day when a girl said that she respected me and I was able to say to myself that I respected me too. I'll always have the day when the captain treated me with justice.

These Things Plus Today

I'll always have the day when the navy wouldn't have me but my mother's mercy told me that there was hope. I'll always have twenty thousand other wonderful days, each of which made my life what it is today. Many of those days would surely be leading candidates to have been my best day so far. But none of them is the winner. Any one of them could be second place.

There is only one day that is my best day so far, and that is today. Today is the day for me to sing "This is my day, my best day so far." And if today is not my best day so far, then I need to repent. I need to sing in the morning and all the day. I need to hear in my heart: "He lives to silence all my fears. He lives to wipe away my tears." He lives to help me do all I need to do to make this my best day so far. I need to walk humbly with my God by talking sincerely about good things with those whom I love. I need to have confidence and start doing some new good stuff. I need to get joy out of doing simple things like walking, feeding animals, and enjoying nature and my own thoughts. I need to find a mountain and climb it all the way to the top, even though it is not a very high mountain. I need to find a newly ploughed field and start planting the seeds of my dreams. I need to be nice to everybody I meet. I need to pray for hope and repent from those things which cause me to despair. I need to stop doing those things that don't cause me to have self-respect and start doing those things that do. I need to treat people with justice even though that is harder on me sometimes than it is on them. And, oh, how I need to be merciful, and when I see that someone is already down I need to not push them further down but rather help them up.

Then when I've done these things, and some other things, things that I will somehow know at the time that I should do, then today and tomorrow and each new day will be my best day so far, and I sure will be happy.

But now it's time to say "I love you, Marilyn"; "I love you, life"; "I love you, my dear Lord." Because this sure is my best day so far.